The Twelve Plays of Christmas

Lillenas **Drama**

The Twelve Plays of Christmas

by Martha Bolton

Lillenas PUBLISHING COMPANY

KANSAS CITY, MO 64141

Dedication

To my soon-to-be-retiring editor,
Paul Miller

Over the years I've had the pleasure of working with
many different editors. Some are business associates,
many are friends. Paul *is* family. He's also a man of
vision, especially in the area of church drama. Without a
doubt, Paul Miller is responsible in large part for many
of the advances church drama has made over the years.
The stage has been, and always will be, a passion of his,
and that passion has clearly shown through his work.
The impact he has made on the management and staff at
Lillenas, drama directors, actors, bookstore owners, and
Christian drama writers everywhere will not soon be
forgotten. I'm grateful to God that our paths crossed.
My family and I cherish his friendship.

Contents

Acknowledgments

I wish to thank . . .

My husband, Russ, who has shared the roller coaster of life with me and never once asked for his money back.

My sons—Russ II, Matt, and Tony—who are a daily reminder of God's countless blessings.

My daughter-in-law, Nicole, for calling me her "best friend."

My granddaughter, Kiana, for letting me know what it's like to shop in the little girls' department.

Paul Miller, John Mathias, Hardy Weathers, and all the wonderful people at Lillenas Publishing Company. They're the best!

And a heartfelt thank-you to the millions of people who every year do their part to keep the spirit of Christmas alive.

The Twelve Plays of Christmas is a collection of sketches and monologues based on the classic Christmas carol "The Twelve Days of Christmas." The scripts are intended to be performed as a full evening of entertainment; however, many of them could also work individually, depending on your needs.

The staging requirements for this production are minimal. Few props are needed and cast size, in most cases, is small. Costuming and set design can be as simple or as elaborate as your drama budget will allow.

NOTE: IF *THE TWELVE PLAYS OF CHRISTMAS* IS PERFORMED IN ITS EN-
TIRETY, AN ENSEMBLE GROUP SHOULD ENTER BEFORE EACH
SKETCH AND SING THE APPROPRIATE LINE OF THE "TWELVE DAYS
OF CHRISTMAS."

ENSEMBLE GROUP *(singing):* "On the first day of Christmas, my true love gave to
me . . . a partridge in a pear tree . . ."

(ENSEMBLE GROUP *exits. Into sketch 1.)*

Up a Tree

5 characters—1 female, 2 male, 1 boy, 1 girl
(The First Day of Christmas)

CHARACTERS:

MARION: *Mom*

KYLE: *Dad*

RANDY: *teenager*

CYNTHIA: *adolescent*

OLD MAN

SETTING: Pine tree forest

PROPS:

> Five or six standing Christmas trees, positioned to look like a pine
> tree forest
> Video camera
> Handsaw
> Toy rifle, should look realistic

COSTUMES: Modern-day cold weather wear

(Sketch opens with DAD, *video camera in hand, backing onto the stage. He's eagerly capturing this "family" moment on camera.* MOM *enters, excitedly waving at the camera. She immediately starts looking over the trees.* RANDY, *bored and carrying the handsaw, enters next, followed by* CYNTHIA.*)*

MOM *(to* DAD): Here . . . over here . . . yoo-hoo! (DAD *aims the camera in her direction.)* That's good . . . Are we rolling?

DAD: You're wasting tape. Say something.

MOM: OK . . . OK . . . *(Excitedly into camera)* Hi! We're here in the Smoky Mountains because this year the Bartleys, that's us, are going to *cut down our very own Christmas tree!*

RANDY *(into camera):* Donations for our bail should be sent to "The Bartley Family Freedom Fund," in care of the local Sheriff's Department.

MOM *(gives a "courtesy" laugh, then edges* RANDY *out of the way):* Always the clown, that one . . . Anyway, I called and got permission from the owner of the land, so this is all on the up-and-up.

CYNTHIA *(excited):* So, which one are we gonna swipe, huh, Mom? Which one are we going to swipe?

MOM *(calmly, into camera):* Apparently, Cynthia didn't hear what Mommy just said. *(To* CYNTHIA) We are not *swiping* a tree, sweetheart. We've got the owner's *permission* to take one.

DAD: I'm gonna run out of tape if you don't hurry.

MOM: Uh . . . yes, well . . . *(into camera again)* . . . as I was saying, we're out here in the middle of the forest in search of the perfect Christmas tree. And the best part is we're doing this *as a family!*

RANDY *(into camera):* Yes, ladies and gentlemen, you guessed it—this is another one of those "family bonding" outings you hear so much about in therapy.

CYNTHIA *(indicating one of the trees):* How's this one, Mom?

MOM: Ummm . . . well, it's nice, but I'd really like one a little bigger.

RANDY: Overkill, Mom. Definite overkill.

DAD: They're all free, Randy. Let your mother get the one she wants.

RANDY: But what's wrong with that one? It's the perfect size. I say let's cut 'er down and go home.

MOM: I want a bigger one.

CYNTHIA *(indicating the biggest tree):* Like this one?

RANDY *(to* CYNTHIA): You gonna cut it down, Paul Bunyan?

MOM: That one's perfect.

RANDY: It's too big, Mom. I'll be sawing 'til New Year's.

CYNTHIA (mockingly): What's the matter? You afraid of getting a wittle ol' splinter in your wittle ol' hand?

RANDY: You know, now that I think about it, I forgot to bring rope for the tree. But, wait . . . that's OK. *You* can just ride outside on the *roof and hold it down!*

DAD: Family . . . family . . . you're not *bonding.*

RANDY: I'd like to bond her mouth with some . . .

DAD (cutting him off): Randy . . . don't forget the tape is rolling.

RANDY: Oh, all right . . . but can't we bond at home in front of a nice warm fire? It's gotta be 20 degrees out here!

CYNTHIA (indicating another tree): Here's a good one.

MOM (she feels it, then shakes her head): Too dry.

RANDY (indicating the smallest tree): This one's the perfect size.

MOM: We're looking for a Christmas tree, Son. Not kindling.

DAD (indicating another tree): Here we go. This is the one.

MOM: Well . . . it's not bad. What do you think, kids?

RANDY: Looks good to me.

CYNTHIA: I like it.

DAD (looks at the back of it): Oh, no . . . it's got a bald spot in the back.

MOM (looks at tree, then at DAD's hair, then back at tree): We don't hold that sort of thing against you, sweetheart . . . You know I'm just kidding.

DAD: I know . . . Well, what d'ya think? We could just keep its bad side to the wall. (Looks at MOM) . . . Don't even say it.

RANDY: It's got my vote.

(Others nod in agreement.)

DAD: Then, let's cut 'er down!

RANDY: Stand back and let me at it!

(RANDY starts "sawing" down the tree as DAD videotapes the event. Meanwhile, an OLD MAN with a "rifle" enters and stands to the side of the stage, aiming it at the family. CYNTHIA sees him, but the others are oblivious.)

MOM (to DAD): I hope the video turns out. I want to send it to Grandma and Grandpa. They'll love watching this. They don't get to see much excitement.

CYNTHIA: Uh . . . Mom . . . uh . . . Dad . . .

DAD: Just a minute, dear . . . Randy, wave at the camera. (RANDY *does so without looking up.*) Can't you show a little more enthusiasm, Son? It's for Grandma and Grandpa. Let them see a little action.

(RANDY *waves again but still doesn't turn around. He continues sawing.*)

CYNTHIA: Something tells me Grandma and Grandpa might get to see a little more action than you planned on.

DAD: What's that, Cynthia? (*His attention is still on* RANDY.) Randy . . . c'mon, turn around and look at the camera.

MOM: Let Grandma and Grandpa see how handsome you are.

DAD: Hurry, Son, I'm running out of tape.

(*Finally,* RANDY *turns toward camera and smiles. He sees the* OLD MAN *with the rifle and freezes like a deer caught in headlights. The others are still oblivious.*)

MOM: Well, I would've preferred a bigger smile, but I guess that's better than nothing . . . All right, Cynthia, now *what* was it that was so important that it just couldn't wait?

CYNTHIA (*motioning in the direction of the* OLD MAN): Him.

MOM: Who? (*Both* MOM *and* DAD *now turn and look.* MOM *gasps.*)

DAD (*panicked):* Don't panic! Don't anybody panic!

MOM: Your father's right. We shouldn't PANIC!

RANDY: You think it's loaded?

OLD MAN: Drop that saw or you'll find out.

DAD (*to family):* It's all right . . . we've got to stay calm. Calm heads always prevail in situations like this.

MOM: Why don't you walk over there, dear, and see what he wants?

DAD: That's what I was just about to say. Why don't you walk over there and see what he wants?

MOM: I should stay here with the children.

DAD: I'm their father. I should stay with them.

RANDY: Is that the man you talked to, Mom?

MOM: He sounded a lot more friendly on the phone . . . Well, Kyle, are you going over there or not?

DAD: You know, maybe we should just get back in the car, drive over to Wal-Mart, and buy one of those plastic trees. They're making them look a lot more realistic these days.

MOM: *Plastic?* Why would I buy plastic when I've got permission to get a fresh tree right from the forest? Now, just walk over there and tell him who we are and what we're doing.

DAD: I'm going. I'm going. *(Cautiously approaching* OLD MAN*)* Uh . . . hi . . . we're the Bartleys. We're just here getting our Christmas tree—you know, it being Christmastime and all. We wanted a fresh one this year, so my wife called and . . .

OLD MAN *(cocks his rifle):* Git off my land!

DAD: You're the owner?

OLD MAN: Been my land for nigh on 50 years! My pappy's land 'fore that.

DAD: Well, apparently there's been some sort of misunderstanding. See, my wife called and talked to . . . well, the owner . . . maybe that was you . . .

OLD MAN: Don't own no phone.

DAD: Maybe it was your son.

OLD MAN: Don't got no family.

DAD: Well, whoever she talked to, they gave their permission for us to take any tree we wanted.

OLD MAN: 'Twern't me she talked to, and the way I see it, you're all trespassing! Now, I told you to git! *(Starts toward* DAD*)*

DAD *(backing up):* Uh . . . yes, well, uh . . . I'm sure we can come to some sort of reasonable . . .

(OLD MAN *walks a little closer, gun still raised.)*

MOM *(to* DAD*)*: Let me talk to him, dear. *(To* OLD MAN*)* . . . Sir, I'm the one who called and . . . well, I don't know who I spoke to, but I promise you I did get permission to take any tree I wanted between River Bend Way and Pine Road. Now, perhaps if you try real hard, you'll remember that conver . . .

OLD MAN *(cutting in):* Lady, you're between Eagle Rock and Oaktree Road. And I ain't never given no one permission to cut down my trees!

MOM: You mean, this isn't River Bend Way?

DAD *(backing up):* We're so sorry, Sir. Obviously, we've made a terrible mistake. You see, we're usually good, law-abiding citizens . . .

OLD MAN: . . . out *stealing* a Christmas tree!

RANDY (*to* MOM): I told you we were going to need bail.

MOM (*to* OLD MAN): We weren't *stealing* your tree, Sir. I had *permission*.

OLD MAN: Tell it to Judge Judy. And anyway, you can't even get to River Bend Way and Pine Road. The roads are closed 'cuz of the snow. If I were you, I'd just turn around and go right back where you came from!

MOM: Without a tree?

OLD MAN: Without buckshot in your britches!

DAD (*to* MOM): He's got a point, dear. Let's just go and leave the nice man alone. I really don't think you're going to change his mind.

(OLD MAN *takes a few more steps toward them both, rifle still raised.*)

MOM: All right, Sir, we're going. We'll get off your land. We'll go home empty-handed, *without* a Christmas tree. But all I can say is . . . (*sarcastically*) I hope you have a very merry Christmas!

OLD MAN: Git, you bunch of tree-thievin' varmits, 'fore I call the sheriff!

MOM: Well! I never . . . !

CYNTHIA: Let's just go.

(*As family begins walking off,* OLD MAN *backs offstage, gun still aimed at them.*)

RANDY: Well, Mom . . . you did it again. Did you ever think you missed your calling? The way you keep almost getting us arrested, maybe you're supposed to start a prison ministry.

MOM: I had *permission*. I don't know who I talked to, but I had *permission!*

DAD: Don't worry about it. He's just a grumpy ol', lonely old man.

CYNTHIA: Yeah. I bet he spends every Christmas all by himself.

RANDY: A loaded rifle tends to cut down on your carolers.

DAD: The quicker we get away from this place, the better!

CYNTHIA: I hope you never end up like that, Dad.

DAD: I don't think anyone intends to end up like that. They just keep shutting people out, one by one, until they're all alone.

(*They walk a few more steps, then . . .*)

MOM: Wait . . .

DAD: Why are you stopping? So he can take better aim?

MOM: Why didn't I see it?

DAD: See what?

MOM: You're right. You're absolutely right.

DAD: As much as I like the sound of those words, what are you talking about?

MOM: That old man. He's going to spend Christmas all alone, isn't he?

RANDY: And I'd like to spend it *alive.* Can we go?

MOM: Don't you think that maybe we're here at the wrong address for a reason?

DAD: Yeah. You're terrible at directions.

RANDY: Hey, why are you feeling sorry for him? We're the ones who don't have a Christmas tree. He's got his pick of any one he wants.

MOM: Which is better—to have a Christmas tree or to have Christmas? Aren't we forgetting that Christmas is about sharing God's love with others? Trees are nice, but we don't need one to celebrate this day. That man needs what we've got a lot more than we need what he has . . . I'm going back.

DAD: I say we just leave well enough alone.

MOM: I can't. *(As MOM walks toward OLD MAN)* Kids, go on and wait for us in the car.

DAD: *Us?*

MOM: C'mon, let's go see if we can talk to him.

(The kids exit hesitantly. MOM and DAD walk toward OLD MAN.)

MOM *(calling offstage):* Sir . . . excuse me, Sir . . .

OLD MAN *(enters, gun still in hand):* I thought I told you to git!

MOM: I had to come back to wish you a merry Christmas.

OLD MAN: Lady, you're really starting to get on my nerves. Anyway, you done wished me one.

MOM: That one didn't count. I was upset. It wasn't in the right spirit.

OLD MAN *(sarcastically):* I hadn't noticed.

MOM: I want to apologize, too, for trying to take one of your trees. I should have checked the street signs better. I'm sorry.

OLD MAN: You're still not getting a tree.

MOM: That's all right. A tree's just a symbol of Christmas. Christmas means a lot more than that. It's the birthday of Jesus, God's only Son, who came down from heaven to prove to the world how much the Father loves us.

OLD MAN: You're not fixin' to preach to me now, are you?

MOM: No, but most people like hearing that they're loved.

DAD: We can live without a tree. But why would you want to spend another day not knowing God's love?

MOM: You know, if you don't have anyone to spend Christmas Day with, we'd like to invite . . . (DAD *gives her an "are you crazy?" look, then relents and nods his head*) . . . we'd like to invite you over to our house.

OLD MAN (*surprised, then . . .*): I like being alone.

MOM: Well, I just wanted you to know you're welcome. (*Extending hand to shake*) . . . Friends?

OLD MAN: Don't push it.

MOM: Fair enough.

(MOM *and* DAD *turn to leave, then . . .*)

OLD MAN: So, why would He do it?

MOM: What?

OLD MAN: Why would God love me?

DAD: Why would God love any of us? But He does.

MOM (*turning to leave*): Merry Christmas.

(OLD MAN *nods, starts to walk away, then . . .*)

OLD MAN: Ma'am . . . ?

MOM: Yes?

OLD MAN: I've shooed a lot of folks away. You're the first ones who ever cared enough to come back.

(*A beat, then . . .*)

MOM: You'll spend Christmas with us then?

OLD MAN: No. But I wanted you to know that.

MOM (*smiles*): Merry Christmas.

(*He starts to return the smile, but just gives a slight nod instead.*)

BLACKOUT

ENSEMBLE GROUP *(singing):* "On the second day of Christmas, my true love gave to me . . . two turtle doves . . ."

*(*ENSEMBLE GROUP *exits. Into sketch 2.)*

Two Turtle Clerks

3 characters—male or female
(The Second Day of Christmas)

CHARACTERS:

> CLERK 1
>
> CLERK 2
>
> HENRY
>
> FRANK
>
> OTHER CUSTOMERS (nonspeaking roles)
>
> VOICE OVER P.A.

SETTING: Department store

PROPS:

> 2 freestanding counters
> 2 cash registers
> Store mike
> Roll of cash register tape
> Carts or shopping baskets
> Doll in box marked "Baby Burps-a-lot" doll
> Robo-Warrior Mechanical Man
> Various other items

COSTUMES: Modern-day wear

(Sketch opens with HENRY *pushing his cart toward the two checkout counters.* CLERK 2 *is waiting on another customer.* CLERK 1 *motions him over.)*

CLERK 1: I can help you here, Sir.

HENRY: Thanks. (HENRY *pushes his cart to her counter.*) I'm late for a Christmas party, so if you could rush this through, I'd sure appreciate it.

CLERK 1: I'll do my best, Sir.

(Takes one item at a time, reads the price aloud, and enters it into the cash register. She's moving slower than molasses on a winter morning. After several items . . .)

HENRY: Is that the fastest you can move?

CLERK 1: Safety first. *(To* CLERK 2*)* Right, Martha?

CLERK 2: She's right, Sir. Why, do you know the number one injury to cashiers is scanner's wrist?

CLERK 1: If we don't do it the right way, we could permanently disable ourselves.

CLERK 2: It's in the manual.

CLERK 1: Page 48, I believe.

CLERK 2: We could show it to you, if you . . .

HENRY: No, no, that's not necessary. I certainly wouldn't want you to do anything that'll cause injury. Just go ahead and do your job.

CLERK 1: That's what I'm doing, Sir. *(Picks up last item in cart. It's the "Baby Burps-a-lot" doll. She looks it over.)* Ut-oh . . .

HENRY: *Now* what's wrong?

CLERK 1: 'Fraid I'm gonna need a price check on your little dolly here.

*(*FRANK *gets in line behind* HENRY*.)*

HENRY *(to* FRANK, *embarrassed):* It's for my niece. *(To* CLERK 1*)* It was $19.99, I'm sure of it.

CLERK 1: Still gonna need a price check. *(Into mike)* Testing . . . testing . . . Price check on "Baby Burps-a-lot" doll.

HENRY: Is this going to take very long?

CLERK 1: It'll take as long as it takes, Sir. You wouldn't want us charging you an incorrect price now, would you?

HENRY: No, I suppose not. It's just that I'm, you know, in this awful rush . . .

CLERK 1: Sir, you're the one who waited until the last minute to do your Christmas shopping. That's not really our problem now, is it?

HENRY: No, I suppose it isn't.

CLERK 1: You just relax, and as soon as I get a price check on your little dolly here, we can proceed.

HENRY (sighing): Get the price check.

CLERK 1 (picking up on his attitude): Sir, there's no reason to get snotty with me. I'm only doing my job.

HENRY: I wasn't getting snotty.

CLERK 1: I definitely detected a certain degree of snottiness . . . Martha?

CLERK 2: You were snotty, Sir.

HENRY: All right, I apologize.

CLERK 1: Apology accepted.

HENRY: What's taking that price check so long?

CLERK 1: Safety first, Sir. You wouldn't want him to trip and fall just running back there to get a price check on your little dolly, now would you?

HENRY: No. And it's not *my* dolly. It's for my . . . oh, never mind. Do you think you could page them again? I really *am* in a hurry.

CLERK 1: Double page?

CLERK 2 (to CLERK 1): He wants you to double page?

CLERK 1: That's what he said . . . Sir, it's not our policy to double page, but if it'll make you feel better. (Into mike) Put a rush on that price check, will ya? The customer's having a hissy fit.

HENRY: I am *not* having a hissy fit!

CLERK 1 (to CLERK 2): . . . Martha?

CLERK 2: Sounds like a hissy fit to me, Sir.

CLERK 1: Do you know, Sir, that you'd live a lot longer if you'd just learn to slow down?

CLERK 2: She's right, Sir. It's been medically proven that people who take life slowly live a whole lot longer than those who just zoom right through it.

HENRY: So, I guess that means the two of you are going to be immortal?

(When they realize what he means, they both give him a look.)

VOICE (over P.A.): Price check on "Baby Burps-a-lot" . . . $19.95.

CLERK 1 (into mike): Got it. Thanks.

HENRY: Finally. Now, just give me my total, and I'll be on my way.

CLERK 1: Believe me, Sir, we don't want to keep you here any longer than . . . Ut-oh . . .

HENRY: What *ut-oh?*

CLERK 1: Out of tape.

HENRY: You're out of tape?

CLERK 1: It'll just take a minute . . . Martha, you got some register tape?

CLERK 2 *(handing her a roll):* Here you go, honey.

(CLERK 1 *starts changing the roll of tape.)*

HENRY: I can't believe this.

CLERK 1: Safety first, Sir. Why, do you realize paper cuts can be very serious?

HENRY: Why? Do you heal slowly too?

CLERK 1: There's no need for sarcasm, Sir.

CLERK 2: I heard of one cashier at the Piggly Wiggly who got a paper cut, it got infected, started oozing, and just as gangrene was about to set in . . .

HENRY: Please . . . I get the picture.

CLERK 2: Well, surely you wouldn't want to expose my coworker here to that kind of risk.

HENRY: No, I suppose not.

CLERK 1 *(finishes with the tape):* There. Now, I'll just have to start over with your order here . . .

HENRY: Start over? Are you kidding?

CLERK 1: You want all your purchases on the same receipt, don't you, Sir?

HENRY: Oh, just forget it. Forget the whole order!

CLERK 1: Even your dolly?

HENRY: I'll just give my niece the cash instead!

CLERK 1: Well, Sir, if that's your decision . . .

HENRY: It's my decision! *(Exiting exasperated)*

CLERK 1: Well, now, you come back and see us again real soon.

HENRY: Don't hold your breath.

CLERK 2 *(waiting a few beats to make sure* HENRY *is out of the store):* So, it worked, huh?

CLERK 1: Like a charm. *(They high-five each other. Then* CLERK 1 *picks up the doll, excitedly.)* The last "Baby Burps-a-lot" doll on the shelf and she's all mine! Every store in town's been sold out of these dolls for weeks! I had this one hid by the automotive supplies, but he must've found it. *(Hands* CLERK 2 *some cash)* Twenty ought to cover it . . . huh?

CLERK 2: That was a close one. *(Rings up the charge and puts the money in the cash register and the doll in a bag)*

CLERK 1: Next . . .

(FRANK steps up to the register and places a boxed "Robo-Warrior Mechanical Man" down on the counter.)

FRANK: I'm kinda in a hurry. Do you think you can rush this through?

CLERK 1: The new "Robo-Warrior Mechanical Man"? Isn't this the toy your son wanted, Martha?

CLERK 2: Yeah, that's it. Where'd you find it?

FRANK: Funny, I looked and looked, but there weren't any on the shelves. Then, while I was shopping over in Kitchen Appliances, I looked behind one of the toasters, and there it was! Strange, huh?

CLERK 2 *(looking guilty):* Yeah. Strange.

FRANK: So, do you think you can you hurry this up? That last customer took so long, I'm way behind on my schedule.

CLERK 1: I'll do my best, Sir. But it's always safety first. *(To CLERK 2)* Right, Martha?

CLERK 2: Right. Why, do you know the number one injury to cashiers is scanner's wrist?

CLERK 1: If we don't do it the right way, we could permanently disable ourselves.

CLERK 2: It's in the manual.

CLERK 1: Page 48, I believe.

CLERK 2: We could show it to you, if you . . .

FRANK: Oh, no, not this again!

CLERK 1 *(looking over the box):* And I'm going to need a price check too.

FRANK: Forget it! I'm going somewhere else! *(He exits in a huff.)*

(CLERK 1 and CLERK 2 wait a few beats to make sure he's out of the store.)

CLERK 2: So, what'dya think? Will $25.00 cover it?

CLERK 1: Twenty-five'll do it. (CLERK 2 *pays* CLERK 1 *the money.* CLERK 1 *puts it in her cash register and hands her the toy.)* Next . . . *(As another customer steps up to her counter, she turns to* CLERK 2.) . . . And who says it's no fun to Christmas-shop?

BLACKOUT

ENSEMBLE GROUP *(singing):* "On the third day of Christmas, my true love gave to me . . . three French hens . . ."

(ENSEMBLE GROUP exits. Into sketch 3.)

A Fowl Battle

4 characters—3 female, 1 male
(The Third Day of Christmas)

CHARACTERS:

LYNN

GLADYS

CARA

JUDGE

SETTING: The 14th annual "Great Hen Cook-off"

PROPS:

Three cooked hens, each on a platter
Glass
Knife and fork
3 entry cards
Freestanding counter
Sign that says "The 14th Annual Great Hen Cook Off"
Wristwatch for JUDGE

COSTUMES: Modern-day holiday wear, casual

(Sketch opens with the JUDGE standing behind the counter, sampling the hens. A sign that says "The Annual Great Hen Cook-off" is either above him or on the counter. Two hens on platters are on the counter in front of him. One hen is quite burnt. There's an entry card in front of both hens. GLADYS and LYNN are standing off to the side.)

27

JUDGE (*hitting the side of a glass with his fork*): Could I have your attention, please? Your attention, please. The moment you've all been waiting for has finally come. It's time to award this year's first place ribbon to the best hen roaster this side of the Rockies!

LYNN (*stepping forward*): That would be *me*.

GLADYS (*pulling her back*): Not so fast, Wolfgang! I'm in this contest too, you know, and my bird hasn't lost a cook-off yet.

(*Throughout the following dialogue, the* JUDGE *continues sampling the birds.*)

LYNN (*indicating one of the entries*): Is *that* your bird?

GLADYS: That juicy, golden brown, taste-bud-pleasing, prizewinning hen right over there? Yes, it's mine.

LYNN (*looking it over*): You're lucky KFC was open today.

GLADYS: Madam, are you accusing me of cheating?

LYNN: If the drumstick fits . . .

GLADYS: I'll have you know I prepared that hen with a recipe that's been in my family for over a hundred years.

LYNN: Are you sure it isn't that hen that's been in your family for over a hundred years? It looks pretty wrinkled and dried out to me.

GLADYS: You're just seeing your reflection off the platter.

LYNN: Well! You're no spring chicken yourself, you know!

GLADYS: No, but I sure know how to cook one.

LYNN: We'll let the judge be the judge of that.

GLADYS (*indicating the other hen*): So is that *your* hen?

LYNN: Yes. Jealous?

GLADYS: I'll say. How come no one told me there was a hummingbird category?

LYNN: That's a full-size hen.

GLADYS: It may have been before *you* got hold of it. A little overcooked, don't you think?

LYNN: I like my hens crispy.

GLADYS: Crispy? Who set the temperature gauge? King Nebuchadnezzar?

LYNN: Say what you will, but my bird's going to be wearing the first place ribbon before this day is through.

GLADYS: The judge may put one on him, but it'll just be to cover him up. He does have his pride, you know.

LYNN: Well, your bird certainly doesn't have a chance of winning.

GLADYS: Apparently you didn't hear what the judge said after sampling my hen last year.

LYNN: It was too hard to understand him with that stomach pump in his mouth.

GLADYS: I'll refresh your memory. He said mine was the best hen he'd ever tasted in his entire hen-tasting life.

LYNN: You say a lot of things when you're delirious from ptomaine poisoning.

(CARA *enters carrying her hen on a platter. She smiles at* LYNN *and* GLADYS, *hands her entry card to the* JUDGE, *then sets her platter down on the counter.*)

CARA (*to* JUDGE): I hope I'm not too late.

JUDGE: Not at all . . . Ladies, it looks like we've got us a late entry.

GLADYS: Is that fair?

JUDGE: According to the rules it is. Entrants have until twelve o'clock to bring in their hens. (*Looking at watch*) And seeing how it's only 11:58, this entry is absolutely acceptable.

LYNN (*to* GLADYS): Disappointed?

GLADYS: No. The more competition the better.

LYNN: It does look pretty good, though, doesn't it?

GLADYS: It doesn't have that nice black color that yours does, but it might still have a shot.

LYNN: What if the judge likes hers best?

GLADYS: Not a chance. My bird's got that one beat wings down.

JUDGE (*samples the new entry*): Oh, my goodness, that's delicious!

LYNN (*to* GLADYS): He's saying that just to throw us off, right?

JUDGE: I have to tell you, ladies, this has been a close contest. All the entries were good, but this year, the first place ribbon has got to go to this late entry. It's the best hen I've ever tasted!

GLADYS: We demand a recount!

JUDGE: I'm the only one voting.

LYNN: Then we demand a recall!

JUDGE: Ladies, ladies, don't be sore losers. Her hen won fair and square.

GLADYS: But I stayed up all night working on my hen.

LYNN: And I've been cooking mine since Tuesday.

JUDGE: Sorry, but I've made my decision. *(Raising* CARA's *hand)* Ladies and gentlemen, it's my pleasure to introduce to you the winner of this year's "Great Hen Cook-off" *(reading off the entry card),* Cara Thompson! *(To* GLADYS *and* LYNN) There's no need to be discouraged, ladies. There's always next year.

(They grumble to themselves as they pick up their hens and start to leave . . .)

GLADYS: I suppose he's right. There *is* always next year.

LYNN: Not for me.

GLADYS: You're not throwing in the towel that easily, are you?

LYNN *(shrugs her shoulders, then as they exit):* But you know, maybe if I lower the oven temperature to say 400 and cook it another couple of days . . .

BLACKOUT

ENSEMBLE GROUP *(singing):* "On the fourth day of Christmas, my true love gave to me . . . four calling birds . . ."

(ENSEMBLE GROUP exits. Into sketch 4.)

Four Calling Birds

4 characters—4 male or female
(The Fourth Day of Christmas)

CHARACTERS:

TARA

NEIL

MITCH

CATHY

SETTING: The telephone company control room

PROPS:

A switchboard
4 headsets

COSTUMES: Modern-day wear

SFX: Telephone ring

(Sketch opens with the four telephone operators at their respective stations. Their headsets are on.)

(SFX: Telephone ringing)

NEIL *(into headset):* Operator . . . Please hold while I connect you to that number. *(Makes a connection on the switchboard)*

TARA *(into headset):* Operator . . . I'll be happy to connect you. *(Makes a connection on the switchboard)*

CATHY *(into headset):* Operator . . . Yes, I can connect you right away. *(Makes a connection on the switchboard)*

MITCH: So, how many families have you united today?

TARA: Fifty-six mothers and sons, 48 fathers and daughters, 37 siblings, 26 couples, and 143 answering machines with 143 answering machines.

(SFX: Telephone ringing)

TARA: I'll take this one. *(Into headset)* Operator . . . Please hold. *(Makes the connection, then to others)* Make that 57 mothers and sons.

CATHY: I think it's sweet when sons remember to call their mothers.

TARA: Sweet, nothing . . . it's *scriptural!*

CATHY: Scriptural? How do you figure that?

TARA: Proverbs 31:28 . . . "her children arise up, and call her."

NEIL: Isn't that "Her children arise up, and call her *blessed"?*

TARA: Maybe. But when I read Bible verses, I just read till they say what I like, then I stop. It's easier on my life that way.

(SFX: Telephone ringing)

MITCH: My turn. *(He answers the call.)* Operator . . . Sorry, but Santa isn't taking calls today. He had some late deliveries last night . . . I can put you through to his voice mail, though . . . Please hold. *(Makes a connection on to switchboard)*

CATHY: So, how'd we all get stuck working on Christmas?

MITCH: I volunteered.

TARA: Volunteered? You've got family, Mitch. Why in the world would you volunteer?

MITCH: My mother-in-law's here from out of town.

(SFX: Telephone ringing)

TARA: I'll get it. *(Answers it and talks inaudibly into her headset)*

MITCH: I've got it all perfectly timed. I get off at eight o'clock. The way I figure it, my mother-in-law'll be in bed and all the toys should be assembled by then.

TARA *(pulls a switch on the board, indicating she's through with the call):* Well, I would have given anything to be with my family today.

NEIL: So why aren't you?

TARA: When you're new, you take what they give you. Besides, it's time and a half. Somebody's got to pay for all this "Joy to the World."

NEIL: Somebody already did.

TARA: Someone's making my MasterCard payments?

NEIL: No. They paid an even bigger debt.

TARA: Nothing's bigger than my MasterCard payment.

NEIL: Don't you realize what Christmas really means?

CATHY: You mean besides all the overpriced merchandise?

TARA: And no parking spaces at the mall.

MITCH: And ungrateful relatives.

NEIL: Christmas is the birthday of one man who forever changed the world—Jesus Christ.

CATHY: We all know that, Neil. But you've got to admit Christmas has come to mean all those other things too.

NEIL: Yes, but it doesn't have to. Christmas is what we make it. If we allow it to be commercialized, then we'll have a commercialized Christmas. But if we want it to be real, we have the power to do that too.

TARA: So, why are you working today?

NEIL: One of the secretaries wanted the day off to spend it with her family. Since my parents are gone now and it's just me, I took her shift. And anyway, maybe I was meant to be here . . . to remind us all that the spirit of Christmas is worth protecting.

CATHY: You know, maybe I should have taken the day off.

TARA: Me too. I don't need the money that bad.

CATHY: I say we all go home and celebrate Christmas right.

TARA: I'm with you!

MITCH: Wait! We can't go! Not yet anyway. My mother-in-law's still up.

NEIL: It's Christmas. Go home and be with your family.

MITCH: All right, but you're coming with me.

NEIL: I couldn't do that. I'd feel out of place.

MITCH: It's OK, really. I'm just kidding about my mother-in-law. She's really not that bad. I'm sure that pit bull she bit last week had it coming.

CATHY: Then it's settled. We're outta here!

(They all start to leave, then . . .)

(SFX: All four lines start ringing at once.)

MITCH: But what about all these calls?

(They look at each other, then at the switchboard, then . . .)

ALL: Let 'em use E-mail!

(They all unplug their phone lines at the same time, then exchange Merry Christmases as they exit.)

BLACKOUT

ENSEMBLE GROUP *(singing):* "On the fifth day of Christmas, my true love gave to me . . . five golden rings . . ."

(ENSEMBLE GROUP *exits. Into sketch 5.)*

Give 'Til It Hurts

5 characters—5 male or female
(The Fifth Day of Christmas)

CHARACTERS:

BELL RINGER 1

BELL RINGER 2

BELL RINGER 3

BELL RINGER 4

BELL RINGER 5

SETTING: In front of a department store

PROPS:

5 kettles with tripods

5 bells

Signs (for BELL RINGER 3) that say "DON'T MAKE ME HAVE TO TAKE IT FROM YOU" and "GIVE OR I BREAK-A YOUR FACE"

COSTUMES:

BELL RINGER 1 is dressed as a Santa.

BELL RINGER 2 is dressed in winter wear.

BELL RINGER 3 is dressed in tough-looking street wear.

BELL RINGER 4 is dressed as an elf.

BELL RINGER 5 is dressed in an authentic-looking charity uniform.

Several extras

(Sketch opens with BELL RINGERS *1, 2, 3, and 4 set up for their collections. Extras enter and walk by* BELL RINGERS. *As they do, the* RINGERS *start a "ring off," trying to outdo each other and get the attention of the extras. It doesn't work. The extras walk on by, not acknowledging them in the least.)*

BELL RINGER 1: Can you believe that?

BELL RINGER 2: This town is full of Scrooges!

BELL RINGER 1 *(turns bucket upside down; nothing's in it):* I've been out here all day. All I've gotten is a chill.

BELL RINGER 3: It's your own fault. You guys are going about this all wrong. You gotta *make* people give to you. You can't offer 'em a choice.

BELL RINGER 2: Forcing people to give against their will? That never works.

BELL RINGER 3: It does for the IRS.

(Another passerby comes along. He takes out a few bills, puts them back, then drops a coin in BELL RINGER 4's *bucket and exits.)*

BELL RINGER 4 *(looking at coin):* Great. Now I can finally go on that cruise to the Bahamas.

BELL RINGER 2: How do these people sleep at night?

BELL RINGER 1: Probably on top of their money!

BELL RINGER 2: Well, if they don't start giving pretty quick, I'm calling it a night.

BELL RINGER 4: I'm with you there.

BELL RINGER 3: So, who are you ringing for anyway?

BELL RINGER 4: The oppressed.

BELL RINGER 3: Bosnia? Sarajevo?

BELL RINGER 4: No. *Me.* My wife cut my allowance again.

BELL RINGER 3 *(to* BELL RINGER 2): How 'bout yous?

BELL RINGER 2: "Holiday Overeaters Anonymous."

BELL RINGER 4: Never heard of 'em.

BELL RINGER 2: I'm the president . . . and the secretary . . . and the treasurer . . . and . . .

BELL RINGER 3: I got the picture. So, how much you got so far?

BELL RINGER 2 *(counting the coins in his bucket):* Fifty-eight cents and . . . *(holding up a paper)* . . . a Little Debbie's coupon.

BELL RINGER 3: I'm tellin' ya, ya gotta be more aggressive.

BELL RINGER 4: I say you need a gimmick.

BELL RINGER 2: Is that why you're dressed like an elf?

BELL RINGER 4: I'm dressed like an elf? *(Thinks for a beat)* . . . No wonder this was on the sale rack.

(BELL RINGER 5 *enters and sets up his bucket and tripod.*)

BELL RINGER 3: Hey, who told you you could set up here?

BELL RINGER 5: The store manager.

BELL RINGER 2: He knew *we* were already out here! What's he trying to do? Drive us out of business?

BELL RINGER 5: Guess he thought there was enough Christmas spirit to go around.

BELL RINGER 3 *(sarcastically):* Yeah, we were just saying how we oughta go get us some bigger buckets.

BELL RINGER 5: Well, I've always found people are quite generous this time of year.

BELL RINGER 2: Well, they're not tossing any of it our way, that's for sure.

BELL RINGER 3: Look, pal, nothing personal, but you're gonna have to beat it. We were here first.

BELL RINGER 5: But I come here every year.

BELL RINGER 3: Don't make me and the elf here have to get ugly.

BELL RINGER 4 *(gives BELL RINGER 3 a look, then):* Yeah . . . don't make us have to get ugly.

BELL RINGER 5: There's no need for us to compete, brothers. I'm sure there's plenty of goodwill around here for all of us.

BELL RINGER 3: You're just not catchin' on, are you? We've been out here all day, and we've hardly raised enough to pay the parking tickets.

BELL RINGER 4: Right . . . *What parking ticket?*

BELL RINGER 3: You own an Isuzu Rodeo?

BELL RINGER 4: Yes.

BELL RINGER 3: A blue Isuzu Rodeo?

BELL RINGER 4: Yes.

BELL RINGER 3: My mistake then. *Your* parking ticket.

(BELL RINGER 4 *looks in the direction of the "street" and reacts as he "sees" his car getting ticketed.*)

BELL RINGER 5: Well, I don't know how much you've raised so far, but I come here every year and thanks to the generosity of these people, our needs are met far beyond our expectations.

BELL RINGER 4: So what's your gimmick? You've gotta have a gimmick.

BELL RINGER 5: No gimmick.

BELL RINGER 3: You scare 'em into giving, don't you?

BELL RINGER 5: Oh, goodness' sakes, no.

BELL RINGER 1: Then, how do you get them to give?

BELL RINGER 5: They just do. I set up here and people stop and give whatever they can.

(*A man enters, walks by the other buckets, then stops and drops some bills into* BELL RINGER 5's *bucket.*)

BELL RINGER 2 (*to* BELL RINGER 5): How'd you do that?

BELL RINGER 1: Yeah, you weren't even set up yet.

BELL RINGER 5: Happens like that every year.

BELL RINGER 2: Oh, go ahead and set up. What's one more bucket?

BELL RINGER 5: Thanks. The Lord's Rescue Squad appreciates it.

(*He starts setting up.*)

BELL RINGER 3: So, that's what you call yourself? The Lord's Rescue Squad?

BELL RINGER 5: That's us.

BELL RINGER 2: Good name. Oughta really tug some heartstrings. So, how much ya rake in in a day?

BELL RINGER 1: For yourself, he means.

BELL RINGER 5: Myself? Oh, no. This isn't for *me*. It's for those who don't have anywhere to go on these cold nights. We provide shelter and food.

BELL RINGER 3: C'mon . . . you can tell *us*. We're all in the same racket.

BELL RINGER 4: It's freezing out here. You gotta be getting a pretty good cut.

BELL RINGER 5: No. Just a warm feeling in my heart.

BELL RINGER 3: You stand out here in the cold every year and you ain't gettin' some kind of kickback?

BELL RINGER 5: Doing for others, isn't that what Christmas is all about?

BELL RINGER 2: Well, yeah, but . . .

BELL RINGER 5: Surely, you're not out here collecting for yourselves.

BELL RINGER 3: My favorite charity.

BELL RINGER 5: But don't you realize you're missing the real meaning of Christmas. Christmas isn't a time to see what we can do for ourselves. It's a time to do for others.

BELL RINGER 2: Well, uh, sure, we knew that.

BELL RINGER 5: It's a time to show how thankful you are for the things you have and give to those less fortunate than you.

BELL RINGER 1: Uh, yeah, well, uh . . . that's the general idea.

BELL RINGER 5: You don't need gimmicks or scare tactics or even an elf . . .

BELL RINGER 4: That's the last time I buy clearance!

BELL RINGER 5 *(continuing)*: You don't need any of those things to make people want to give to you. All you need is a just cause, the right motive, and watch the donations start pouring in.

(As BELL RINGER 5 starts ringing, passersby drop in dollars and coins. BELL RINGERS 1, 2, 3, and 4 watch in amazement, then gather up their belongings, take the money out of their buckets, and drop it in BELL RINGER 5's bucket. Satisfied, they take their tripods, their empty buckets, and they exit.)

BLACKOUT

ENSEMBLE GROUP *(singing):* "On the sixth day of Christmas, my true love gave to me . . . six geese a-laying . . ."

(ENSEMBLE GROUP exits. Into sketch 6.)

A Change of Plans

A monologue
(The Sixth Day of Christmas)

CHARACTER:

GILBERT

SETTING: Meeting room for the Fraternal Order of Geese No. 873

PROPS:

Poster board
Easel
Marker

COSTUMES: A simple (beak and a few feathers) or an elaborate goose costume

(Monologue opens with GILBERT standing at the easel and poster board, marker in hand. The poster board should have a formation design drawn on it.)

GILBERT: You all know why we're here today. Winter's coming and we need to decide if it's going to be the same-o, same-o fly-south-for-the-winter kind of thing, or are we once and for all going to have the courage to try something new? Will we be bold? Will we be daring? Will we ignore our instincts, forget tradition, and do something wild for a change? After all, who among us REALLY wants to fly south for the winter . . . AGAIN? Flown there—done that. It's time we tried something different. It's time we went where WE want to go! It's time we flew west for the winter. I've always wanted to see Disneyland anyway! Or east! Do you know how many statues are in Washington, D.C., alone? It's a pigeon's paradise! Or we could even fly north. Penguins don't get a lot of company. So what are we waiting for? Sure, there are only six of us here tonight, but I know I speak for the rest of the flock! It's time to do our own thing! Break out from the crowd! Let those other birds fly south if they want, but I for one have had it up to here *(indicates)* with all that salsa and that south-of-the-border cuisine! So, all in favor of embarking on a new adventure this winter, raise your right wing . . . No one? Not one of you is willing to break away from the flock? All right, be that way! I'll send you a postcard from Disneyland! *(Starts to fly off toward the west)* No, on second thought, D.C. sounded pretty good. I'll call you from atop the Jefferson Memorial. *(Starts to fly off toward the east)* North . . . that's where I'm heading. Those penguins know how to party! *(Starts to fly off toward the north, then turns and looks back)* . . . So, that's it? You're all still gonna fly south? . . . Oh, all right, I'll go with you. But I'm tellin' ya, this is the *last* year! *(As he "flies" toward the south)* Don't think I'm going to do this all through the new millennium! *(Grumbling to himself)* South . . . I can't believe we're flying south again! Well, I'm not wearing the sombrero, I'll tell ya that. I liked to never got off the ground with that thing. And they better not put chili pepper in the birdseed again. It'll keep me up all night. And another thing . . .

BLACKOUT

ENSEMBLE GROUP *(singing):* "On the seventh day of Christmas, my true love gave to me . . . seven swans a-swimming . . ."

(ENSEMBLE GROUP *exits. Into sketch 7.)*

Singing in the Rain

4 characters—female
(The Seventh Day of Christmas)

CHARACTERS:

CAROLER 1

CAROLER 2

CAROLER 3 (leader)

4 CAROLERS (singing parts only)

ELDERLY LADY

SETTING: Front door of a house

PROPS: 7 umbrellas

COSTUMES: Rain gear

SFX:

Rain

Thunder

(Sketch opens with CAROLERS *standing at the front door of a house. Their umbrellas are open, and they're singing the ending line of a Christmas carol. We hear the sound of heavy rain throughout the entire sketch, as well as thunder where indicated. Following song . . .)*

CAROLER 1: Whose idea was it to come Christmas caroling on a night like this anyway?

CAROLER 2 *(sneeze):* Mine, I think.

CAROLER 1: Don't you ever watch the Weather Channel?

CAROLER 2: Yes, but you've forgotten something, sister.

CAROLER 1: Yeah. My wet suit.

CAROLER 2: You're forgetting that we're not out here doing this for *our* comfort. We're doing this to bring a little Christmas joy to *others*, to spread peace and goodwill to those who need it most. Sister, *this* is a *ministry.*

CAROLER 1: I see. We get 'em out here, get 'em saved, then we baptize 'em on the spot? Anyway, I don't think anyone's home. They would've come to the door by now.

CAROLER 2: Well, we'll soon find out.

CAROLER 3 *(to group):* OK, ladies . . . "We Wish You a Merry Christmas" on three.

CAROLER 1 *(to* CAROLER 2): You'd better not hold your head back when you hit those high notes. You could drown!

CAROLER 3: And a one, and a two . . . and a . . .

CAROLERS *(singing):* "We wish you a merry Christmas / We wish you a merry Christmas / We wish you a merry Christmas / And a happy new year!"

(The others stop singing, but CAROLER 1 *continues.)*

CAROLER 1: "Now bring us a life preserver. / Now bring us a life preserver. / Now bring us . ."

CAROLER 3: Hey, those aren't the words.

CAROLER 1: A little rewrite.

CAROLER 3: You can't rewrite a classic. Now, let's try it one more time.

(Leading the CAROLERS)

CAROLERS *(singing):* "We wish you a merry Christmas / We wish you a merry Christmas / We wish you a merry Christmas / And a happy new year!"

CAROLER 3: Good. Good.

CAROLER 2: I still say they're not home.

CAROLER 3: They're probably just getting dressed. What shall we sing next?

(SFX: Loud clap of thunder)

CAROLER 1: Well, "Silent Night" is out.

CAROLER 3: This is quite a storm, isn't it?

CAROLER 1: I say we mail 'em a Perry Como CD instead.

CAROLER 3: She might have a point.

CAROLER 2: You're not wimping out, are you, sisters?

Caroler 1: No, but do you still have that fruitcake you brought?

CAROLER 2: Yes. Why? Are you hungry?

CAROLER 1: No. But in case the dam breaks and floodwaters start heading our way, I wanna make sure we've got something heavy enough to anchor us.

CAROLER 3: Maybe we'll just sing one more song and then go.

CAROLER 2: How 'bout "It Came upon the Midnight Clear"?

(SFX: Another clap of thunder)

CAROLER 3: Maybe not.

CAROLER 2: I can't believe you're all afraid of a few little sprinkles! *(Singing)* "It came upon the midnight clear . . ."

(SFX: Thunder)

(One by one, the CAROLERS singing along)

CAROLERS: "That glorious song of old."

(SFX: Thunder)

CAROLERS: "From angels bending near the earth / To touch their . . ."

(SFX: Thunder, the loudest yet, along with a heavy downpour of rain)

CAROLER 2: OK, maybe a Perry Como recording would be just as good.

CAROLER 1: Race you to the van!

CAROLER 2: You're on!

CAROLER 3: Wait for me!

(All the CAROLERS race offstage.)

(SFX: Storm slowly tapers off to just a light rain)

ELDERLY LADY *(opens door)*: Funny . . . I was sure I heard singing out here . . . Probably just my imagination. *(Singing softly to herself)* . . . "to touch their harps of gold. / 'Peace on the earth, goodwill to men, / From heav'n's all-gracious King.' / The world in solemn stillness lay / To hear the angels sing."

BLACKOUT

ENSEMBLE GROUP *(singing):* "On the eighth day of Christmas, my true love gave to me, eight maids a-milking . . ."

(ENSEMBLE GROUP exits. Into sketch 8.)

Stable Duty

3 characters—2 female, 1 male
(The Eighth Day of Christmas)

CHARACTERS:

ABIGAIL

EUNICE

SHEPHERD 1

SHEPHERDS (extras, nonspeaking roles)

SETTING: Outside of a stable in Bethlehem

PROPS: 2 buckets

COSTUMES: Bible time clothing

(Sketch opens with ABIGAIL onstage walking toward stable, bucket in hand. She's obviously exhausted. EUNICE enters, bucket in hand.)

EUNICE: Good morning, Abigail. You're getting an early start today, aren't you?

ABIGAIL *(half asleep):* Uh . . . huh.

EUNICE: It's amazing how many people have come to our town, isn't it?

ABIGAIL: Uh-huh.

EUNICE: Hundreds. Even thousands. I've never seen so many strangers.

ABIGAIL: Uh-huh.

EUNICE: Well, you're certainly not much for conversation this morning.

ABIGAIL: Ut-huh . . . Sorry. I'm just tired.

EUNICE: So, where are all the others?

ABIGAIL: If they're smart, they're still in bed.

EUNICE: They can't sleep all day. Their cows have to be milked too.

ABIGAIL: All I know is I'm milking mine, then going right back to bed!

EUNICE: Didn't you sleep well last night?

ABIGAIL: Not a wink.

EUNICE: It wasn't our guests who kept you up, was it? A few of them were pretty rowdy.

ABIGAIL: No. That wasn't it. It was this couple . . . they came by looking for a room. I felt terrible. I had nothing to give them.

EUNICE: A young couple?

ABIGAIL (nodding): And she was with child.

EUNICE: Yes, yes . . . I know who you mean. They came by our inn too. But I had to turn them away.

ABIGAIL: I started to, but then . . . well, you know, her being in her condition and all, I just couldn't do it. I offered them the stable.

EUNICE: They took it?

ABIGAIL: They were happy to have shelter. But I couldn't sleep all night knowing they were out there.

EUNICE: Do you think she's had the baby yet?

ABIGAIL: Not in the stable. I hope not. A baby should be born in a house.

EUNICE: None of my babies let me pick where they were to be born.

ABIGAIL: Babies do have a mind of their own, don't they? (Stopping at the door of the stable) I don't want to disturb them, but I've got to milk the cows.

EUNICE: Go on. They'll understand.

(ABIGAIL opens the door to the stable, releasing a blinding light. ABIGAIL steps in to the stable and the light, then rushes out excitedly.)

ABIGAIL: Eunice! Come quick!

EUNICE (runs to stable door): What is it?

ABIGAIL: The baby! He's here! (As they both look through the door of the stable) He's in the back . . . over there, sleeping in our manger.

EUNICE: I see him. He must've been born last night!

ABIGAIL *(bursting with excitement):* I've got to tell someone! I'm a . . . now let me figure this out . . . I'm not his grandmother, and I'm not his aunt. But I must be something! I'm a . . . I'm a . . . oh, for goodness' sakes, what are you when a baby is born in your stable?

EUNICE: I'd say you're blessed.

ABIGAIL: That's it! I'm blessed! I'm blessed! I'm blessed! I'm blessed! *(Several* SHEPHERDS *enter.)* Sirs, I must tell you the good news! A baby was born in my stable last night!

SHEPHERD 1: Yes, we know. An angel told us He'd be here.

ABIGAIL: An angel?

SHEPHERD 1: He said we'd find the Baby, the Savior of the world, lying in a manger in Bethlehem. We've come to worship Him.

(SHEPHERDS *enter the stable, while* ABIGAIL *ponders the moment . . .)*

ABIGAIL: Imagine that . . . the Savior of the world born in my stable and lying in my manger.

EUNICE: You really are blessed, Abigail. You really are blessed.

BLACKOUT

ENSEMBLE GROUP *(singing):* "On the ninth day of Christmas, my true love gave to me . . . nine ladies dancing . . ."

*(*ENSEMBLE GROUP *exits. Into sketch 9.)*

Holiday Workout

2 characters—male or female
A monologue
(The Ninth Day of Christmas)

CHARACTERS:

AEROBICS INSTRUCTOR

BAKER

SETTING: Health club

PROPS:

Cake, not in a box
Order form

COSTUMES: Workout wear

(Sketch opens with AEROBICS INSTRUCTOR *leading the "class" in aerobics.)*

INSTRUCTOR: All right, ladies, listen up! So you overdid it again this Christmas. You ate all eight slices of that pumpkin pie in one sitting and sprayed the entire can of whipped cream directly into your mouth. You drank enough eggnog to clog every artery in your body. And you couldn't stop at just *one* gingerbread house. Nooooo. You had to go and eat the *whole neighborhood!* Now you're feeling a little guilty, a little bloated, a little like . . . well, like curling up with a box of sugar cookies and eating yourself into a post-holiday coma. Don't do it! Blowing your diet during the holidays is a common problem, but it's not the end of the world. It just means you have to work a little harder, that's all. Eight popcorn balls?—50 jumping jacks.

A pan of brownies?—30 minutes on the treadmill. Two quarts of banana pudding?—110 push-ups. See, it's not so bad. Now, let's go. Let's start shedding those holiday pounds. *(Starts doing jumping jacks, as he counts off . . .)* One, two, three, four . . . *(Stopping suddenly)* Mary Beth! Drop those Twinkies . . . I know you're not using them as weights. You're not fooling me. I can see the teeth marks in them from here . . . Now, we'll have to start all over . . . *(Resumes doing jumping jacks)* One, two, three, four . . . *(Stops suddenly again)* Laurie! Empty out those pockets! . . . Don't play innocent with me. Either those are cookies in your pockets or your hips are getting awfully lumpy . . . Yeah, I thought so. Toss 'em . . . All of them . . . All right, is there anyone else who smuggled in their own bakery, or can we continue with our workout? . . . OK now, let's try this again. *(Resumes the jumping jacks)* 1, 2, 3, 4 . . .

(BAKER *enters, cake in hand.*)

BAKER: Where do you want me to put this?

INSTRUCTOR: What are you doing? I didn't order a cake.

BAKER: Well, someone did. *(Reading from order form)* Someone ordered a Death by Chocolate Triple Layered Creamy Rich Dream Cake.

INSTRUCTOR: Oh, it must be for that New Year's Eve party they're having tomorrow night. Just set it in the kitchen.

(BAKER *exits.*)

INSTRUCTOR: All right, girls, let's get back to work. *(Starts doing jumping jacks)* Let's forget all about that triple layered . . . death by chocolate . . . creamy rich . . . moist and tender Dream Cake in the . . . oh, I give up! You can't start working off the holidays 'til after New Year's! What was I thinking? *(Running offstage)* . . . Last one to the kitchen has to do the dishes!

BLACKOUT

ENSEMBLE GROUP *(singing):* "On the tenth day of Christmas, my true love gave to me . . . ten lords a-leaping . . ."

(ENSEMBLE GROUP *exits. Into sketch 10.)*

Return to Sender

3 characters—male
(The Tenth Day of Christmas)

CHARACTERS:

DIRECTOR

BUBBA: *the bigger and burlier, the better*

FRED

SETTING: The annual Christmas program

PROPS:

One bunny costume in a shipping box
Director's chair

COSTUMES:

DIRECTOR: modern-day wear

BUBBA: pink tutu, tights, and leotard

FRED: lord costume

(Sketch opens with DIRECTOR *onstage, sitting in his director's chair.)*

DIRECTOR: C'mon, people . . . we don't have all day! *(Rising, he claps his hands several times.)* C'mon, c'mon, c'mon!

FRED *(enters):* I'm afraid we can't start yet.

DIRECTOR: *I'm* the director. I'll say when we start, and I say we start *now!*

FRED: OK, but we're short a lord.

DIRECTOR *(not really hearing him):* I can't believe these people, trying to tell me how to do my . . . *(Suddenly, to* FRED*)* What do you mean, we're short a lord?

FRED: The song calls for ten lords a'leaping, right?

DIRECTOR: Yes.

FRED: We have nine.

DIRECTOR: Nine?

FRED: Nine.

DIRECTOR: That's it! I quit! I can't work with amateurs! I am a *professional.* I can't deal with these distractions! I . . . I . . . *so where is he?* Where's the tenth lord? Stuck in traffic somewhere? Out leaping with some other drama troupe? Where is he? Has he even called?

FRED: Oh, he's here, Sir. He's just having a little trouble with his costume.

DIRECTOR *(sighs):* Well, at least he's on the premises . . . Well, what are you waiting for? Go tell him to hurry up! We need to rehearse this number and move on! *(Clapping hands)* Let's go! Let's go! Let's go!

FRED: But . . .

DIRECTOR: What's the problem *now?*

FRED: He'd kinda like to . . . well, he'd like to talk to you first, Sir.

DIRECTOR: Fine . . . tell him as soon as he gets out here on the stage, he can talk to me all he wants.

FRED: Well . . . Sir . . . that's just it . . . he'd rather you come to his dressing room.

DIRECTOR: His dressing room? What kind of a prima donna is this guy? I don't have time for this! Tell him he's got 30 seconds to get out here or I'm replacing him! *(Under his breath)* Temperamental actors!

FRED: But . . .

DIRECTOR *(counting):* Twenty-nine, 28, 27 . . . !

FRED: All right, all right . . . I'll tell him . . . but he's not going to be happy.

DIRECTOR *(as* FRED *exits,* DIRECTOR *mumbles under his breath):* Amateurs! I could've been working on Broadway with *professionals,* but no, I had to volunteer to work with . . .

*(*BUBBA *enters wearing tights, shirt, and a tutu.)*

BUBBA: Uh, I think we've got a problem, Sir . . .

DIRECTOR *(turns and sees him; indicating tutu):* What is *that?*

BUBBA: That's what I wanted to tell you. Evidently, there's been a mix-up in the costumes.

DIRECTOR *(frustrated):* Oh, this is just *great!* This is just *perfect!* It's two hours 'til showtime, and I've got nine lords a'leaping and Bubba the Ballerina! . . . Well, it's too late to do anything about it now, you'll just have to go on like that.

BUBBA: Are you *crazy?* I can't go on like this! There are video cameras out there! Bob Sagat would pay big bucks for footage like this! And so would . . . *(name pastor, youth pastor, or other church member's name).*

DIRECTOR: You *have* to go out there. You're under contract.

BUBBA: I didn't sign any contract. This is volunteer, remember.

DIRECTOR: Oh, yeah. Rats! . . . Well, I can't just have *nine* lords. The song calls for nine ladies dancing and *ten* lords a leaping. If you don't go out there, it'll mess up the whole number! People know how to count, you know.

BUBBA: Sorry, but I'm not letting anyone see me in this. I'd never live it down!

DIRECTOR: Work with me here, Bubba. I've got a show to put on. Work with me!

BUBBA: Hey, I know my lines. I'll go on, but I'm not wearing *this.*

DIRECTOR *(calling offstage):* Prozac! I need my Prozac! (FRED *enters carrying a shipping box.)* . . . I don't think I need *that* much.

FRED: This just arrived from Acme Costume Company.

DIRECTOR *(taking the box):* Oh, thank goodness!

BUBBA: My costume?

DIRECTOR *(handing* BUBBA *the box):* Here. Go change and let's get this show on the road!

BUBBA: See, it all worked out. *(As he starts to walk off, he opens the box.)* Oh, no!

DIRECTOR: *What's wrong?*

BUBBA *(pulling bunny costume out of the box):* You know, on second thought, maybe this tutu isn't so bad after all.

DIRECTOR *(collapsing into director's chair):* I wonder if Spielberg ever has days like this!

BLACKOUT

ENSEMBLE GROUP *(singing):* "On the eleventh day of Christmas, my true love gave to me . . . eleven pipers piping . . ."

(ENSEMBLE GROUP *exits. Into sketch 11.)*

Time and a Half

2 characters—1 male, 1 female
(The Eleventh Day of Christmas)

CHARACTERS:

CLARA

CLARENCE: *the plumber*

SETTING: CLARA's kitchen

PROPS: Plumber's toolbox and tools

COSTUMES: Modern-day wear

SFX: Doorbell

(Sketch opens with CLARA *onstage, cleaning the kitchen. The doorbell rings.* CLARA *opens the door and sees* CLARENCE, *toolbox in hand.)*

CLARA: Oh, I'm so glad you're here! I didn't think I'd ever find a plumber who was working today. You were the 11th one I called!

CLARENCE: So, what seems to be the trouble?

CLARA: My garbage disposal. Something's clogging it up, I guess.

CLARENCE: I'll have a look-see.

*(*CLARENCE *goes to the kitchen sink and starts checking it out. He continues to work on the problem throughout the following.)*

CLARA: I hope it's nothing serious.

CLARENCE: The most painful part will be my bill.

CLARA: That's what I'm afraid of.

CLARENCE: I'll work as fast as I can. I'm sure you have a houseful of company coming.

CLARA: Naw. Ain't no one I care to invite.

CLARENCE: No family?

CLARA: None that I speak to.

CLARENCE: I know how that goes. Had a falling out?

CLARA: You ever heard of the shoot-out at the O.K. Corral? We could've gotten along that well but only after years of therapy.

CLARENCE: So where do they live, your family?

CLARA: Sister's 'bout a block away. Got two brothers in the two counties over.

CLARENCE: You're that close and none of you talk?

CLARA: Not directly. But I keep up with them. Read the obituaries, so I know they're still around.

CLARENCE: You know, Ma'am, it's none of my business, but it's not healthy to be holding a grudge this long.

CLARA: Yeah, well, you don't know my family.

CLARENCE: They were pretty mean to ya, huh?

CLARA: Must've been. Can't really remember what they did. But I know it sure made me mad.

CLARENCE: You know, I like to think of grudges like the food in this drain. If we're not careful, they'll just keep piling up and piling up until nothing, not even good stuff, can get through.

CLARA: Yeah, well, you may know plumbing, but you don't know . . .

CLARENCE (*cutting in*): I know you miss them. It's written all over your face.

CLARA: Miss 'em? I don't even remember what they look like anymore.

CLARENCE: I bet you've still got pictures.

CLARA: Yeah, but I cut out all their faces. Anyway, if they want to see me, they know where I live.

CLARENCE: Maybe you have to make the first move.

CLARA: I'm tired of making the first move.

CLARENCE: You called me, a total stranger, and welcomed me into your home on Christmas Day. How hard could it be to call someone you grew up with?

CLARA (*after a few pensive beats*): You done with that disposal yet?

CLARENCE: She's all fixed. Good as new. Now how 'bout repairing something more important. (*Hands her the phone*)

CLARA: You're pretty pushy for a plumber.

CLARENCE: What can I say? My business is fixing things.

CLARA (*she starts to take the phone, then stops*): I'll think about it. I won't make any promises, but I'll think about it . . . So, how much do I owe you?

CLARENCE (*tears up bill*): Not as much as you owe yourself. Make the call.

CLARA: But . . .

CLARENCE: Merry Christmas.

CLARA: You can't do that.

CLARENCE: I own the company. I can do whatever I want. I'll just gather up my things and be on my way. (*As he collects his tools*) . . . You know, I don't have any family left, but if I had another chance to be with them, I sure wouldn't waste a minute.

CLARA: Thanks . . . (*indicating bill*) for this.

CLARENCE: You know, you have the right not to call them. But is that really what you want? (*As he's leaving*) You have a good one now . . .

(CLARA *shuts the door behind him and walks over to the sink and starts cleaning. She glances toward the phone, walks over and picks up the receiver, then hangs it up and resumes cleaning . . . until finally, she picks it up again and starts to dial . . .*)

BLACKOUT

ENSEMBLE GROUP *(singing):* "On the twelfth day of Christmas, my true love gave to me . . . twelve drummers drumming . . ."

*(*ENSEMBLE GROUP *exits. Into sketch 12.)*

A Different Beat

2 characters—male or female
(The Twelfth Day of Christmas)

CHARACTERS:

DRUMMER 1

DRUMMER 2

10 extras (nonspeaking)

SETTING: Annual Christmas program

PROPS:

Twelve snare drums (at least two should be real)
Twelve sets of drumsticks

COSTUMES: Festive drummer wear

(Sketch opens with DRUMMERS 1 *and* 2 *standing center stage, wearing their snare drums, drumsticks in hand.)*

DRUMMER 1: C'mon, dude. I haven't eaten all night. How many more times are we going to practice this?

DRUMMER 2: Until you get it right. Now, let's try it again. *(Singing as he beats the drums)* "O come, all ye faithful . . ."

DRUMMER 1 *(beating his drums while he sings off-key; his timing is way off too):* "O come, all ye faithful . . ."

DRUMMER 2: Stop! Stop!

DRUMMER 1: Was I off again?

DRUMMER 2: Can a fruitcake survive a nuclear disaster? Of course you were off!

DRUMMER 1: But I'm getting closer. Close is good, isn't it?

DRUMMER 2: Ask Shorty Matthews.

DRUMMER 1: Who?

DRUMMER 2: Shorty Matthews. A high diver at my school who used to think *close* was good enough.

DRUMMER 1 *(cringing):* Don't tell me he . . .

DRUMMER 2: . . . missed the pool by about four inches. Went from 6'3" to 5'1" in one dive.

DRUMMER 1: Ouch.

DRUMMER 2: Right. So, shall we try to get a little closer? *(Sings)* "O come, all ye faithful . . ."

DRUMMER 1 *(beating the drums; is off again):* "O come, all ye . . ."

(Once more DRUMMER 2 *reaches his hand out and stops him.)*

DRUMMER 1: Still off?

DRUMMER 2: It's your timing. To put it in musical terms, it . . . it, well, it *stinks!*

DRUMMER 1: It does? *(Looks hurt, then)* Oh, I get it. That's one of those *hip* words, like when you say someone's bad but you really mean they're good.

DRUMMER 2: No. I meant you really . . .

DRUMMER 1 *(continuing in his own world):* Wow, thanks, dude! No one's ever said my drumming *stinks* before. That's awesome!

DRUMMER 2: C'mon, let's just try it again.

DRUMMER 1 *(he beats the drums and sings again, but there's not much improvement):* "O come, all ye faithful . . ."

DRUMMER 2 *(trying his best to stay calm):* Can I ask you something?

DRUMMER 1: It's a natural talent . . . Is that what you were going to ask?

DRUMMER 2: No. I wanted to ask how you got cast for this part in the first place.

DRUMMER 1: Beats me. I was just delivering pizza this afternoon and they said they were short a drummer.

DRUMMER 2: All right, then. So you were cast in the usual way. But when you read the script, didn't you figure it'd be a good idea to know how to play the drums—seeing how this is the "Twelve Drummers Drumming" sketch and all?

DRUMMER 1: I figured I'd pick it up at rehearsals. And it's working. Even you said I stink.

DRUMMER 2: Maybe I should just cut the song.

DRUMMER 1: Cut the song? You can't do that. It's the big finale.

DRUMMER 2: Eleven days . . . 12 days . . . who'll know the difference? Most people only know it up to the five golden rings anyway. Or maybe I'll just cancel the show altogether.

DRUMMER 1: You can't cut the song. And you can't cancel the show. You think I stink now? If we keep practicing, I'll show you how I can *really* stink. I'll stink so good, or bad, or however it is you hip dudes say it, that record companies will be lining up to sign me!

DRUMMER 2: You're willing to keep practicing until it's perfect?

DRUMMER 1: All night if I have to. The pizza's cold anyway.

DRUMMER 2: Well, maybe if we work into the night . . .

DRUMMER 1: I won't let you down, man. Anyone who believes in my talent the way you do deserves my best stinking performance!

DRUMMER 2: I'd be happy if you just sing on key and stay on beat.

DRUMMER 1: Like this? (*He beats the drum and sings, only this time he's sounding a little better.*) "O come, all ye faithful . . ."

DRUMMER 2: Hey, that's not bad.

DRUMMER 1: "Joyful and triumphant . . ."

DRUMMER 2: Good. Good. Keep it up.

DRUMMER 1: "O come ye, O come ye . . . to Bethlehem."

DRUMMER 2: Hey, you just might work out after all.

(*As* DRUMMERS 1 *and* 2 *sing and play the second verse, the other 10* DRUMMERS *begin to enter, drumming and singing along with them.*)

ALL: "For He alone is worthy. / For He alone is worthy. / For He alone is worthy. / Christ, the Lord."

DRUMMER 2: Hey, I think you've got it!

DRUMMER 1: Well, it just goes to show ya—you can do anything if you just put your mind to it.

DRUMMER 2: Well, I guess it also doesn't hurt that this is the night for miracles.

DRUMMER 1: So, the show's going on?

DRUMMER 2: Of course it is! The show *always* goes on!

(Entire cast enters and joins them onstage, singing "The Twelve Days of Christmas.")

ENTIRE CAST:

> *On the twelfth day of Christmas*
> *My true love gave to me*
> *Twelve drummers drumming . . .*
> *Eleven pipers piping . . .*
> *Ten lords a-leaping . . .*
> *Nine ladies dancing . . .*
> *Eight maids a-milking . . .*
> *Seven swans a-swimming . . .*
> *Six geese a-laying . . .*
> *Five golden rings . . .*
> *Four calling birds . . .*
> *Three French hens . . .*
> *Two turtle doves . . .*
> *And a partridge in a pear tree!*

DRUMMER 1 *(does a final drumroll, then proudly):* I'm *really* stinking now!

THE END